Bilberry Pie
and other tasty tales

by the

Egton Bridge Writers' Group

Fryup Press

Published in June, 2006
by
Fryup Press, Bracken Hill, Glaisdale
Whitby, YO21 2QZ

ISBN Number 0 - 9545951 - 1 - 4

© The Egton Bridge Writers' Group

Cover Design & Photographs Ann Bowes

Other photographs
Members of the Egton Bridge Writers' Group

Illustrations by Judy Rawlinson

Printed in Great Britain
by
York Publishing Services
York

INTRODUCTION

'The Egton Bridge Writers' Group began in 2001, one of three groups set up by the Open University, as part of a widening participation initiative in rural North Yorkshire. Initially, sponsorship came from the Post Office (then Consignia). When funding stopped and the planned sessions finished, the writing continued.....'

ACKNOWLEDGEMENTS

The writers would like to thank Richard Weightman, Helen Berry, Matt Parsons, Peter Godbold, Elizabeth Waters, Trevor Johnson, Anthea Ellis and others who helped us in the application process to raise funds in order to publish this book.

We are very grateful to our combined sponsors - The Scarman Trust, Scarborough Borough Council, the Moors and Coast Committee of North Yorkshire County Council and Awards for All – for enabling us to produce the first anthology of our work.

Finally, thanks are due to Bob Rawlinson and Ken Trewren for additional photographs and for the patience of our families while we grappled with our writing!

EGTON BRIDGE WRITERS' GROUP

Pat Almond

Ann Bowes

Pat Henderson

Jean Ramsdale

Judy Rawlinson

Kate Trewren

CONTENTS

Spirit of Place
Bilberry Pie 1
Bridge of Love 4
Late Snow 7
Melting Tar and One-Eye. 10
Garlic for Breakfast 13
Snow Lessons 14
Dry-stone Waller 17
Gooseberry Capital of England. 18
Showtime 20
The Lily Pond 21
Life's a Bitch 23
The Last Jumble Sale 25
Whitby Tales of Terror 28
Ode to the River Esk 30

Colourful Characters
In the School Psychologist's chair 31
Magic Kit 33
Changing Times 35
Snowy 36
No Job too Small .38
The Pheasants 41
Fruit Baskets 43

Thoughts from Abroad
Where the Water Meets the Sky 45
Venice - 'La Serenissima' 48
To Rome and Back 51
The State of Florida 55

Fancies, Friends and Feelings
The Little Blue Book of Autographs 57
Singing 59
Games We Played 60
Tomorrow will You Remember 61
Words of Consolation 62
On Listening to Wagner 63
How Do I? 64

"A marvellous freedom from the tumult of the world."

St. Ailred of Rievaulx Abbey, 1143, speaking about the North Yorkshire Moors.

"No vision of Yorkshire would ever be complete without the freedom, wildness and romance of its moors."

SPIRIT OF PLACE

Bilberry Pie

Ann Bowes

Doris struggled for breath as she hurried up the steep footpath, the bracken on either side catching on her basket. She knew she should have left sooner but Ralph had pleaded with her to stay another few minutes. She never complained when asked to take the cakes and pies over to her aunt's in the next valley, for it meant she could see her friend on the way back. Her mother would never have approved of their illicit friendship, Ralph not knowing who his father was and besides, her mother thought fifteen far too young to have a boyfriend.

As she reached the brow of the hill, her worst fears were confirmed – the old green Dales bus was disappearing round the bend in the road. Doris sighed as she stopped a moment to get her breath back. Oh well, she'd have to walk. It would soon be coming in dark but she knew she could find her way over the rigg and she might just get home about the same time as the bus. It had to travel a long way down the valley, wait in the village a while and then continue up the next dale, where Doris lived with her mother and father.

She ran down the slope, crossed the road and found the track leading up to the moor. She would have to go through Hangman's Wood. It would take too long to go round. In the summer, she often walked over the rigg when she visited her aunt but always avoided the wood for it spooked her. Old Bertram, who lived in the cottage, was said to be just a bit weird. The hand-gate into the wood was all tied up with string so she scrambled through the hedge at the side, tearing her skirt on a briar. She would have to think of some explanation for that when she got home.

It was eerie and almost dark under the canopy of trees as she made her way along the path. An owl startled her as it hooted. It was muddy in places and slippery where pine needles littered the damp earth. She was nearing the cottage when she tripped on a fallen branch and stumbled to the ground, catching her hand on a sharp stick. She yelled instinctively and immediately a dog started barking. She crouched low, scared stiff, hoping the dog was tied up. She could feel her heart thumping. Then she heard a gruff voice shouting.

"Who's there?" several times. The dog continued barking but didn't sound any closer and after a few more shouts all went quiet. Knowing she'd have to hurry she stood up and cautiously made her way along the path and when she was out of earshot of the cottage ran to the end of the wood, almost tripping again.

Her heart was still pounding as she climbed over the wall onto the safety of the moor. Out of the wood it wasn't quite so dark and she found the well-used sheep track up the hillside. She recognised familiar rocks and gullies as she scrambled passed bracken patches and heather beds to the open moor. It was cooler here and a mist was descending as darkness fell. She reached a boundary stone and could make out the outline of the first shooting butt so knew now she wouldn't get lost.

She made her way from butt to butt, counting them as she did so. She was nearing the last one in the row when she heard voices approaching. Men's muffled voices. Terrified, she hurried to the butt and crouched down inside. She was unaware of the damp grass and the stones of the butt sticking into her back. The voices sounded closer and she could make out odd words here and there. Curiosity got the better of her and she slowly stood up, peeping through the heather covering the top of the butt. Dimly she could make out two figures, jacket hoods pulled over their heads. They were each carrying a spade and between them, a large sack.

"This'll do, she'll be happy with this spot," said one. The other had his back to Doris and she couldn't catch his reply. They were about twenty yards from her hiding place. They laid the bundle down and started digging.

"Careful wit' sods - have to put 'em back just same."

Doris was petrified and daren't move. She watched, horrified as they dug a deep hole, then lifted the sack and laid it in the grave. After replacing all the soil, they meticulously put back each heather-clad sod.

"It'll soon settle and rain'll wash away any bits of soil," the first man said, adding, "Jake Thornton will never know. Nor anyone else." They shook hands, picked up their shovels and disappeared into the fog.

Jake Thornton was the Gamekeeper and Doris knew he was not well liked. He shouted at anyone he found on his moors, threatening them and once took someone to court for trespassing. Shivering, Doris picked up her basket and left the butt. She picked her way across a bilberry bed and headed down into the slack, following the course of the stream in the bottom until she reached the track leading to her home. She could see the welcoming lamplight flickering through the window and hoped her father wasn't around. Her clothes were damp and her short hair clung to her brow, wet from the fog.

"Look at you girl, you're all wet and what happened to your skirt?" asked her mother. "Quick and get changed before your father gets back. Why are you so late?"

"The bus was late," Doris lied. "Auntie loved the bilberry pie and ginger cake. Said she'd been a bit better this week. Where's Dad?"

"Down in the village. Old Mrs. Theaker's still missing. Police have been round asking questions. Your dad was the last person to be seen at her cottage. Now be sharp, off you go." Puzzled, Doris picked up a candlestick from the shelf and after lighting it from the fire, went upstairs. Thoughts whizzed round her head as she changed. She knew her dad had a temper but surely, he wouldn't harm anyone? Especially Mrs. Theaker. Why, her dad was a friend, often taking her old spaniel out! She'd said Zipper missed going on the moors after her husband died. People said she was worth a bit but no-one really knew. They never had a car. Even her dad had a car, one of the first people in the village to get one. Doris remembered when he'd taken Mrs. Theaker to the hospital when she'd broken her wrist. She jumped off her bed. That was the car outside. She tiptoed downstairs, then paused as she heard her mother's voice.

"Did you get it done?"

"Aye, fog came just right." Doris froze. Her dad? And her mother *knew*? She didn't know what to do. What could she do? She'd pretend she hadn't heard. Might be safer all round. She went in, closing the door behind her and blew out her candle. She placed it on the shelf, avoiding their looks. Better say something, she thought.

"Have they found Mrs. Theaker yet?" Her parents looked at each other and then her father spoke.

"No, not yet. They're organising a search party in the morning."

After tea Doris said she was tired and went to bed early. What a day! She was so confused and had had two very frightening experiences and daren't say anything. She slept and dreamt her father was chasing her through Hangman's Wood with Zipper, and old Bertram was shouting and laughing in a weird way, waving a stick at them.

Next morning the fog had gone and sunshine was streaming through the window when Doris entered the kitchen. Her mother smiled, as if everything was normal.

"Are you all right dear, you look a bit peaky?"

"Yes, just had a bad dream." Suddenly, her father burst through the door, beaming.

"Good news. They've found her. After Zipper died she decided to visit a long lost sister and never told anyone. Johnson took her to the station and stayed with his daughter a couple of nights. Just got back this morning." He paused. "What's the matter Doris?" She was standing open-mouthed, appalled at what she'd been thinking. She managed to stammer something.

"I, er.. was thinking, er… I didn't know about Zipper," she finished lamely. Her mother smiled.

"Well, he was quite old and he's in the best place now!"

The Bridge of Love (fabrication and legend)
Pat Henderson

Tom Ferres was awakened by a shaft of daylight which crept slowly across his face. It was still early and the north east wind had a sharp bite to it but Tom had chores to do before having this day away from work to visit the annual St. Hilda's Fair at Whitby. Raising himself from the palliasse he felt the straw filling scratch his naked torso but today it didn't seem to matter. Pulling on his breeches, he climbed quietly down from the loft and let himself into the yard. Grabbing a clean sack he walked across to the pump, placed the shirt he had slung over his shoulder onto a convenient nail and, as the water gushed from the spout, held his head into the stream. It was icy cold. He washed, sluiced the water through his hair and grimaced as it trickled down his back but a brisk rub with the sack warmed him again and, as he walked towards the cottage, he pulled on his shirt and yanked his braces into place. This morning he and his father had to count and check the sheep up on the moor before he could even think of leaving for the Great Fair.

Glaisdale bordering on Egton was a fair march from Whitby and later he joined the people walking from his village, those from Egton, Lealholm and others, all joyfully making their way towards the fun of the fair. Once in Whitby, would he be able to spin a stone into the North Sea and watch the ripples on the water or behold the boats anchored offshore or tied up in port? How he dreamed of sailing on a ship to far off lands!

With much good humoured jostling and pushing, at last Tom gained entrance to the fair and after a comforting tot of rye whisky, feeling relaxed and happy, he was drawn to the sound of music. Leaning against a balustrade he watched as couples gaily attempted a gavotte. He tapped his toe in time to the music and cheekily winked at a pretty wench, who looked bored as she tried to keep in step with an elderly man. As the music drew to a close he managed to manoeuvre his way to the girl's side and begged for the honour of the next dance. As it finished, he knew he was totally smitten. He bowed, escorted her from the floor and begged to be allowed to know her name. She told him she was Agnes Richardson and that she came from the Glaisdale area. Her father was Squire Richardson, a wealthy landowner, who disapproved of any poor man who wished to court his fair haired daughter.

Meeting secretly, Tom and Agnes fell deeper and deeper in love until Tom could stand the hidden trysts no longer. He went to ask for Agnes's hand in marriage. Scornfully, the Squire repulsed him and forbade the couple to ever meet again. Agnes was distraught and begged Tom to try once more. The angry answer was the same but to appease his sad daughter he reconsidered, should Tom Ferres ever become a rich man, the squire would then give his daughter his blessing and consent to the marriage.

Nightly, Tom would walk to the bank of the River Esk and, peering through the valley mist, seek out a lighted lamp in Agnes's window which signalled they could meet. Stepping stones were the only way to cross the river and in darkness this was perilous. Always the thought of holding his beloved in his arms spurred Tom on. When the river was in spate all contact was impossible, and he vowed that should he return a rich man he would build a bridge to allow future lovers the chance to cross safely.

The time arrived for Tom to leave the moorland village and seek his fortune. Volunteers were needed to defend the land against the Spaniards and enthusiastically he offered his services. Bad weather made farewell to Agnes impossible and, without even saying goodbye, he had to leave for Plymouth to board the merchant ship St. Hilda.

Tom gained much respect for his navigation skills and, although storms delayed battle with the Spanish Armada, victory was accomplished with great dexterity. Tom proved fearless throughout and won praise from Sir Francis Drake, later sailing with him for the West Indies. He was made captain's lieutenant when the St. Hilda plundered Spanish galleons and filled the holds with treasure. Hurricanes and tornadoes battered the ship but Tom seemed to revel in the adverse conditions. He even took possession of a larger ship into which the treasure trove was transferred.

The time had come to sail for Britain. He had been away from his homeland and his adored Agnes for several years and yearned to see both again. With his pockets full of gold he knew that at last he could claim her hand in marriage. He increased his fortune still further in

London by selling the captured ship and then travelled to Whitby, where, from the assembled crowds, he received the welcome of a hero. The treasure was divided, thus making Tom a richer man than his future father-in-law.

Agnes was as beautiful as ever and Tom, brimming over with love and longing, swept her into his arms. Together they approached her father, this time confident that their marriage hopes would be fulfilled. Squire Richardson could no longer procrastinate. Seeing the happiness in Agnes's sparkling eyes, he gave his blessing. Glaisdale celebrated the uniting of Tom Ferres and Agnes Richardson before the church altar and all rejoiced that the story had such a happy ending……
The end - well almost … Tom and Agnes chose Hull for their marital home and, in that busy port, Tom took a substantial interest in the shipping business but he had one final promise to fulfil. True to his word, a stone bridge was built over the River Esk between Glaisdale and Egton…… Beggar's Bridge.

There is debate as to whether Tom Ferres was actually born in Egton or the neighbouring village of Glaisdale or even Lastingham. However, exist he did. Different versions of this romantic story will always be told and be as captivating and beautiful as the Beggar's Bridge itself.

Late Snow

Pat Almond

On Valentine's day in Rosedale Abbey the sun shone on the early daffodils and the sky was blue. The following Monday the school was closed because of snow. Such is life at the southern end of the North York Moors.

Rosedale Abbey lies like an upturned cup in a cleft of hills and seems to have a microclimate all its own. On this Monday even vehicles with four wheel drive were troubled by the snow that had blown in overnight. A way out had to be found. For the eldest children from the village primary school this was the day they had looked

Lake District on an outdoor activity holiday. It took the combined efforts of two Land Rovers, a tractor, a harassed teacher or two, four snow-crazed eleven year olds and a set of determined parents to deliver the children to the main road to catch the bus for Humphrey Head. They were just two hours late and this was the last snow they were to see all week.

At the first hint of snow or icy conditions the bus company that collects the secondary children from the dale cancels the coach. The prospect of treacherous Cropton Bank looms large and a bonus day with no school is a much-welcomed perk for teenagers living beyond Hartoft and Lastingham. After the first hour or two the novelty wears off and the village boys scramble and slither across the ruts and slush to congregate at the 'little school'. As eleven year olds they long to move on to Pickering. As twelve year olds the village school is the first place they return to when they are at a loose end. The hope is always that the primary school will be open so that they can strut their freedom just beyond the gate that corrals the infants and junior children. Once lessons resume, and the younger ones go inside, the boys enter the playground sliding and pivoting their bikes in extravagant manoeuvres whilst the little ones gaze in wonder and longing from the classroom windows. Inevitably the riders are sent away but they have registered their presence, impressed their former classmates and they usually wander home satisfied. On this Monday they had no audience for the primary school was deserted.

On Tuesday the school reopened with just sixteen pupils in attendance. Those from isolated farms stayed at home, preferring to be snowed in there rather than face the possibility of being snowed in at school should more showers arrive. The Land Rover that serves as a school taxi brought in six children from Rosedale East – a ten year old boy and five little girls. They trudged in a line across the playground with their heads down against the wind. The pink and blue of the girls' clothing was garish against the sea of white. Their faces were solemn and their steps reluctant. As they reached the small cleared area near the door all the accumulated snow from the roof above shivered in a heap to the floor. It showered the boy from head to foot without touching one of the girls. They dissolved into gales of laughter as did those watching from inside. Rueful, but smiling, the victim led his troupe into the warm building.

Inside, with their Wellingtons paired and dripping on sheets of newspaper, the children absorbed the novelty of being part of the small group who had made it to school. Odd ones straggled in over the first hour and work began, though there was little urgency and there was a relaxed feel about the group gathered in one room with plenty of adult attention and companionship. An improvised timetable invigorated the learners and the day passed quickly. The coldness of the wind and the depth of the accumulated snow outside meant that drawing, Lego and Connex were the order of playtimes. Knowing that hometime was close the children were dismissed from lessons early to play together, warmly wrapped, in the snow for a while before going home. A series of snowmen began to appear. One wore a traffic cone for a hat, one a little pink bonnet. 'That one's for Beth's little sister' they explained. In the staffroom the visiting doctor and school nurse on annual reviews watched anxiously as odd flakes drifted from snow heavy skies, they too fearing they could be marooned in the village.

In the playground the boys became noisier and then a little bolder as they played, lobbing lumps of snow at the wall. 'No Snowballs!' they were told. Little by little they began again, surreptitiously flicking small handfuls of snow at one another. 'No Snowballs!' It took at least another two reminders before the culprits skulked away looking aggrieved, to kick at the deep drifts in the church gateway. Two tiny infants played king of the castle on and off a deep tub topped with snow. Under the snow and their feet, were lines of small bright flowers that had cheered the playground days before. Eventually the taxi and cars began to arrive to take the children home. The younger ones wore pinched expressions and were pink with cold, their shoulders hunched against the wind and their eyes streaming. The older ones laughed and shouted to one another as they left the yard. In just a couple of minutes it was deserted save for the surviving snow people.

Wednesday was the same as Tuesday with just fourteen children. On Thursday the snow was waist deep in places. An RAC man trapped in his van overnight in a road leading out of Rosedale Abbey made the national news. The school was closed. It reopened on Friday and sixteen children did lessons as the snow turned to sleet and the dripping thaw set in.

On Monday normal schooling resumed and the four adventurers, on their return from Humphrey Head, were told about all the fun they had missed.

Melting Tar and One-Eye

Jean Ramsdale

Finding the photos after forty years brought it all back to me. Riding my *Jack Taylor* handmaid racing bike over the North Yorkshire moors has provided me with unforgettable memories.

The rides were always well-planned, with a small off-shoot group from the Co-op Cycling Club. We weren't the fastest or the most professional but we seemed to have the fun-times. I was proud of my silver and black lightweight cycle. It had an aluminium water bottle, quick-release wheels, one carrier for absolute necessities and shiny steel toe clips. These clips were essential for pressing your toes (inside leather cycling shoes of course!) forward to sway from side to side in an endeavour to labour up the tough hills. First off the bikes were scorned. The cruel gradients had even the lads defeated on the last haul.

The best times were in summer with a blue sky, hot sun and the promise of a dry base to pitch our tiny bivouacs. The snag with hot summer rides was melting tar. The narrow moor roads then were not so smoothly covered with tarmac. The surface was rough and tar oozed through the gaps to make our cycling a labour of love. The wheels clogged up with the gunge, including tiny gravel particles. It did provide the excuse for an extra stop to get out the oily rags (always carried) and spend ten minutes enjoying the sun as we kept our wheels wheeling! There was no stopping for drinks until we reached camp. However, our water bottles, fixed on the handlebars, had plastic straws and this enabled us to drink 'on the pedal'.

Everything on these glorious trips was down to basics. Our kettle was hidden in the gap of a dry stone wall and the teapot was an Oxo tin. We had more than one site but the kettle and teapot stayed in the favoured Baysdale Beck spot. This place was endowed with springy turf and a clear stream running down through stern grey boulders. The tiny tents resembled a ring of mushrooms and they seemed hardly big enough for elves. However, we only had to crawl in (with most of our clothes on) and kip down for six or seven hours.

Then, it was strictly sleeping alone. You would have had to be a contortionist to accomplish anything but sleep. Once darkness descended and the solitary silence of the moors closed in, there was nothing for it but to crawl in with your bicycle lamp and fall asleep. One night I awoke and felt a presence. My fears welled up and the silence then felt deafening. I lay petrified as the shuffling and heavy breathing, just outside the thin walls of my bivouac, came nearer. My shelter rocked and swayed and I trembled. I felt for my bike lamp and daren't switch it on. What if these noises were from ghosts? There was a ruined Baysdale Abbey and I'd heard that the monks and nuns had enjoyed some riotous times for which they'd been severely punished. Were they coming to stop us from following the same sinful path? Holding my breath was becoming painful. I raised my arm and hurled my lamp towards the tent entrance. Then silence returned. Had I annihilated the ghosts?

Sleep was impossible now and I lay trembling until the light of dawn encouraged me to poke my head outside. Well, what a wally I had been. Why didn't I think of stray sheep wandering down to the beck? I could see two of them balefully eyeing my dishevelled appearance. They must have been curious about what was under the mysterious mushroom shapes. No-one said anything about ghosts or bumps in the night, so I kept my mouth shut!

Talking about sheep brings back memories of One-Eye. He was a pet and for about two years grazed at Baysdale Beck. One-Eye was a loner and invariably appeared as we were freewheeling into the valley.

The author with 'One-Eye'

Could he smell our scent? He became our friend and would put his front hooves onto our chests and expectantly wait for his reward. We started to cater for him when we packed our provisions. Tasty Cornish pasty portions or brown bread and chopped ham were eagerly chomped and swallowed. For his own sake we had to ration food and his one good eye would fix itself into your gaze and look pleadingly for a sign of weakness. But, we had our own needs such as digging out the kettle and erecting the 'throne'.

An important ritual when setting-up camp was, of course, toilet arrangements. We were always a mixed group and sharing 'facilities' was acceptable. Our code name for 'facilities' was 'throne'. This seemed logical as nature deigned we sit on the throne every day (if you were personally designed for once a day). The foundations for this royal seat were left permanently in place. After each Baysdale 'holiday' we carefully dismantled the layers of turf which had formed the top of the throne and replaced them into the ground to regenerate. After about two hours' hard work we had our latest version, fitted into a hollow so that our dignity was preserved.

During the day we left our campsite (nothing to steal there) and, anyway, we were usually the only souls about, except for One-Eye. He would be waiting patiently as we cooked breakfast and who could not feed him when that one eye was steadfastly staring at us? Riding along the moor roads with food in our stomachs and fresh air in our lungs was the life for me. Work in a stuffy office seemed far away and the joys of the moment were intoxicating.

Inevitably, the summer ended. We missed our camping so much that we organised the next best thing, our Sunday rides. On fine winter's days we would be off again, a small 'pack' of cyclists bunched up on the moor roads, the wind whipping around us. There was a magic on the moors in winter. The colours of the sky were special and blended with the shades of terrain. It was nippy and we did not linger on these rides. However, it was all worth it as the feeling of glowing good health and camaraderie was unforgettable.

Garlic For Breakfast

Pat Henderson

"We might as well run a B & B - at least we'd make some money!" I groan at the thought of the washing and ironing after yet another one night stopover. Our house guests throughout the year are numerous, partly our own fault we admit. Hubby and I do enjoy welcoming our lovely family, wonderful friends - old and new, friends of friends and mere acquaintances. They descend on us like the leaves in autumn. We befriend strangers at airports, on flights, on ferries, at hotels and B & Bs and convert them to the delights of North Yorkshire. The Christmas card list lengthens each year and the diary fills rapidly with invitations handed out in eager anticipation of proving to these new (and old pals) just how lovely it is up here and how much we will enjoy taking them to interesting places. Doesn't matter that we've been to the Abbey on average once a fortnight for the past five years, added our pennyworth about Dracula, battled through the tourists in Whitby and Goathland - must see where Heartbeat is filmed, do we know any of the cast? - to Robin Hood's Bay and all points north, east, south and west.

A few of our guests have really stamped the card of memories....Just this year we have welcomed a couple who live down the lane from our daughter in Florida. They were on the big 'tooor' of Europe and just had to see where we lived in li'l ol' England. For two days we drove them to historic sites and beauty spots and in that time Gloria never ceased talking, even to draw breath. Total strangers were trapped and mesmerized as she cornered them, divulging her latest tidings during the next half hour, her patient husband just shrugging and uttering "that's Glawria!" Still, we all had a good time and were sorry to see them leave.

Recently my cousin's Thai wife and son descended for a week.. Hubby and I were to meet their train at Darlington....train arrived...no Anya or Dong emerged.....hell, now what do we do....another train in half and hour. Success this time. From then on Anya took over the running of our house.

"I cook for you, you have rest. I good cook!" (I already knew that, but that's in *her* kitchen). "We eat mussels! You have mussels?"

"Noooo....no mussels, we not buy mussels." I begin to talk like her again, much to hubby's amusement. I've tried to explain it assists Anya if I leave out non-essential words.

"I buy mussels, we go shops. I buy chilli, coconut milk, white wine, garlic and basil, OK?" Anya gives me a hug as she rattles off her list…. I can't feel miffed for long!

The day Anya and Dong were to return home she decided on a cooked breakfast… Fine, I actually had a pack of bacon and a box of mushrooms in the fridge and Anya already knew where the frying pan lived. She fried the whole pack of bacon and then came the mushrooms and *garlic*.

"Garlic for breakfast! Anya, no, not garlic for breakfast." My face was a picture of disbelief.

"Garlic good in mushrooms, very tasty, you see. You have red wine left from last night?"

"Nooo…..sorry, red wine finished last night, but you not put red wine in food for breakfast."

"Aaaah … red wine good in mushrooms," Anya admonished. Silly isn't it, but I could without doubt feel the stirrings of rage within my breast. Hubby said he thought I might detonate any moment and signalled calm down. Composure returned and though I didn't eat the garlic mushrooms and bacon (well, how could I?) the other three tucked in. I very fond of Anya and her abundantly (s)mothered son Dong, but I chief cook in my kitchen - oops, there I go again!

Well, guess I'd better get some clean sheets on the beds and start a shopping list. Who is it coming next? That's nice. Wonder if they would like Whitby kippers for breakfast?

Snow Lessons

Judy Rawlinson

If it snows overnight in our valley, mornings are magical. A white duvet covers everything, muffling all sound. There's no traffic for nothing can get up or down the steep banks. If you strain your ears you can hear the distant roar of the river. It looks so beautiful, so pristine, like an Alpine resort before the skiers arrive.

Ferocious icicles fringe the roof, trees glisten with diamonds and the sharp edges of crags are softened into blancmange curves. White paths through the woods are spattered with red husks of haws and hips where marauding, hungry birds have pecked seeds out of the berries.

Then the fun starts. Here comes the first snowplough-toting tractor to clear the road. Out come shovels and brooms to clear doorsteps and drives or to excavate the car, sitting under a chunk of icing. People spread grit from the neat piles by the roadside, removing spadefuls so that they turn from molehills to frogs with gaping mouths.

We can't get to work on time, if at all, ferry the kids to school or drive to the shops. The children are delighted and, in no time at all, drag their sledges up the hill to whizz down the village's personal Cresta Run. We don't possess a sledge but my big kids (aged 28, 26 and 50 plus) have improvised by filling fertilizer sacks with blankets and carpet underlay to pad their bottoms. I ring the stables two valleys away to say I can't get over to ride today. Are they snowed in? Yes. Are the horses still inside their cosy loose boxes? No, they get frustrated if they are kept inside too long and bang with their hooves on the door. They don't mind snow but hate driving wind and rain. As if to prove a point, round the corner trots a pony and rider, towing not one but two girls on skis.

Things are coming to life now. Gears grind, wheels spin, engines moan. Here comes the first tractor with its black silage bag, now the milk tanker. Animals have to be fed, milked and mucked out. The geese next door are fed up: their pond is frozen but the muddy little spring still flows to supply their drinking water. It's so cold that the river has nearly frozen over, apart from a narrow, fast-slowing channel in the middle.

Outside the kitchen window the blue tits are chomping through the peanuts a mile a minute and the robin is mugging a chaffinch on the bird table. The latter knows when he's beaten and retires to the ground, hopping about in search of leftovers. A large flock of fieldfares and redwings descends on the overgrown hawthorn hedge in the field, stripping it of berries in record time. The dog takes a look outside, confused. Where's the lawn gone? She leaves her calling card in a footprint. More shovelling. A puffed-up robin sits in a patch of sunlight, defrosting.

"It's chaos in town," says the butcher, who's delivering our meat in his trusty van, bless him. "It's like a frozen sea in the high street. They've made no effort to clear it."

He's right, I find out later. The pedestrianised town centre is in a state, a mixture of frozen hummocks, deep slush, icy pools and skating rink. A little boy and his gran pick their way gingerly through this lot, clinging to one another. I'm not sure who's supporting who. There's

an unexpected 'whoomph' as a raft of snow avalanches off the roof of the baker's shop. The customers inside jump.

"Eee, imagine if that had fallen on you, our kid!"

I stock up on a few items, including essentials for my friend up the hill who is still marooned at the end of along, snow-blocked drive – milk and ferret food! Of course, we are secretly proud of our battle with the elements. Down south, a fine sprinkling of snow on the M25 and people can't cope, the wimps. We mustn't complain. It's all a question of flexibility, of rising to the challenge.

One friend, a trainee teacher, was delivering a carefully prepared lesson to a class of infants when it started to snow. The children rushed excitedly over to the window, enthralled as the snowflakes came thick and fast.

"Wow; miss, look at that!"

"Can we build a snowman?"

"I wonder if our Dad will get over the moor?"

Try as she might, Wendy could not get her class to concentrate on the task in hand. She had lost control. Dispirited, she told her supervisor about this afterwards.

"Well, dear," said the supervisor, "you should have given them a Snow Lesson!"

Dry-stone Waller
Ann Bowes

To him each stone's a piece of natural beauty.
Viewed, admired and held in high esteem.
There'll be a place for each and every one
Of them within his architectural scheme.

No mortar or cement he'll need to use,
His eye will tell him where each one will go.
As they interlock like pieces of a puzzle,
He will build them neatly, row on row.

The clang of metal upon stone will ring out clear
As his hammer chips away a needless part.
A string, stretched taut, will be his guiding line
And his finished wall will be a work of art.

The Gooseberry Capital of England
Pat Almond

The first thing I learned about Egton
When I visited long ago
Was that the key to fame and honour
Lay in Egton's superior show.

It doesn't feature fuchsias,
No jam or veg displayed,
Just rows of gleaming gooseberries
Waiting to be weighed.

I vowed to grow a big one
To win that coveted prize
For the greenest, roundest gooseberry
Of a clearly superior size.

I studied growing goosegogs
As a budding champion should
And I borrowed my Dad's recipe
Of sheep dockings and bullocks' blood.

I inherited some bushes
And bought in several more.
I nurtured and I watered them
With evil-smelling gore.

I dreamed down the row of budding stock,
As the emerald leaves unfurled,
That for one whole day in Egton Bridge
I'd be queen of the gooseberry world.

By late July I'd got one –
A winner, it was clear.
I covered it, protected it,
No other fruit came near.

But on the day of staging
I found that I was cursed.
When I went to pick my gooseberry
My big fat fruit had burst!

Had some blaggard rural pricked it?
Or sprayed with killer stuff?
I'd have to wait another year
To have a gooseberry big enough.

But when I called in at the show,
Watched them judge with weights and rules,
It became quite clear my entry
Would have proved me a gooseberry fool.

My wasted, busted goosegog,
A stunner to my eye,
Was a miniature, miniscule effort
Fit only for a pie.

♦ ♦ ♦ ♦ ♦ ♦ ♦ ♦ ♦ ♦

Showtime

Judy Rawlinson

One August day, come rain, come shine,
The goosegog growers stand in line
To show their berries, plump and fair,
Just like the maidens you'll find there.
Men stream in through the schoolyard gate,
Their precious berries on a plate.

The schoolroom's hushed as judges roam
To pick the best ones. What rich loam
And tender care has brought them far
For folk to marvel? From the car
The ladies bring in cakes and tea,
A raffle prize and Auntie V.

One hundred years or more, 'tis said
The gooseberry show has seen fruit bred
To huge proportions. Pink and green,
With yellow veins and mauve we've seen –
Amazing, big as any plum!
I think I'll take some home for Mum.

The air is tense, each dish is set
Upon the snowy cloth. I bet
That gardeners' hearts are fluttering now
To see who'll win and take a bow.
The suns sets and the brass band plays.
The champion grower's in a daze.

Fred never thought his fruit was best
In show. Time for a well-earned rest.
The raffle's called, the prizes won,
Time to relax and have some fun.
To chat to friends or have a beer,
That's it, now, for another year.

♦ ♦ ♦ ♦ ♦ ♦ ♦ ♦ ♦ ♦

The Lily Pond

Ann Bowes

Less than a mile from the village of Danby there is a quiet peaceful little valley, whose stream starts its life up on the Danby low moors. A small farmhouse called Clitherbecks nestles near the top of the valley and fields on either side slope down to the stream. Further down there are wooded areas including sycamore, birch and oak, shrubs and patches of bracken lying either side of the stream as it makes its way to join the River Esk. The farm and the moors surrounding it belong to Lord Downe, whose main residence is at Wykeham Abbey, near Scarborough but for centuries his predecessors had a second home called Danby Lodge which sits at the bottom of the small valley.

Several years ago the property was sold to the North Yorkshire Moors National Park and is now a visitor centre to where many people come to explore and enjoy this beautiful part of North Yorkshire. One of the many walks from the centre leads up the Clitherbeck valley and passes close to the stream. I'm sure many of the visitors will have noticed the small man-made weir in a bend in the stream but not realized its significance, for on the other side, long overgrown and forgotten, was the outline of a once much admired Lily Pond.

In years gone by, the Lord Downe of that time, with his invited guests, their wives, butlers, maids and chauffeurs would come and stay at the Lodge during the grouse shooting season. While the gentlemen went off with their guns and dogs to the moors, the ladies were left to amuse themselves. One of their favourite excursions was to stroll through the fields up the valley to the Lily Pond, sheltered by the aspens, birch trees and rhododendron bushes. Here they would spend happy hours in this haven for wildlife, enjoying their picnic lunch in peace and tranquillity.

Having discovered the history of the place, my husband, an employee on the estate, was set on restoring the pond to its former glory. With the necessary approval, he hired a small mechanical digger and, with the driver, set about cleaning out the brambles, undergrowth and excess soil which had accumulated over the years. The embankment round the stream side of the pond was still there but needed strengthening in places with the excavated soil. In the centre was an island where a silver birch was growing, which they left. Above the weir they discovered a sunken, rusted metal pipe, which had obviously

The Lily Pond, restored to its former glory

been there to feed water into the pond. It was completely blocked with earth. At the opposite end they found another pipe in the embankment, put there to take excess water back into the stream, which was damaged and needed replacing. When all was ready they began to unblock the pipe. Working on the pond side first, they bored out as much soil as they could then, working in the stream, finally forced a way through, producing a trickle of water. Gradually it became a steady stream and finally water gushed forth, spreading across the bottom of the pond.

Two days later the pond was full and the excess water was returning to the stream through the replaced pipe at the far end, so not interfering with the natural flow yet keeping the pond water fresh. And so a dream had been fulfilled. Though the grand ladies of the manor will not return, I hope the Lily Pond and its beautiful surroundings will be there to be admired and enjoyed for many generations to come.

♦ ♦ ♦ ♦ ♦ ♦ ♦ ♦ ♦ ♦

Life's a Bitch

Judy Rawlinson

I'd been going through a bad patch just before we came up here. The last place we'd lived in was spacious enough – big garden, nice house, French windows overlooking the lawn where I could watch the squirrels cavorting. However, the village was boring, far too boring for a country girl like me, brought up on a pig farm. Same old neighbours, same old walks and no swimming once I'd been caught trespassing in the manor pond. I got into big trouble over that. I don't know why they worried. I would never have got near those ducks: there was so much weed, I was hardly able to make any headway. No game birds to speak of, either, very few rabbits, the odd muntjac deer and one exciting episode when a fox ran through the garden and hounds followed it. I was itching to join in.

I was lonely, with the adults out at work all day and the kids away at college. My one companion was the black cat (always good for a game) until he got sick and died. I flirted with Sox, the lurcher and the King Charles over the road but he was such a wimp and refused to come exploring. I did toddle off to the pub for a bit of company and go on solitary dawn excursions, checking out the dustbins. One day I overdosed on takeaway curry outside the village hall after an Indian extravaganza and was whisked off to the vet's for a stomach pump. Very nasty. I was well and truly grounded after that.

My health hadn't been too good, in general. I hated being taken to the vet, even though he was very careful when he removed a grain of corn that had become lodged deep in one ear and said I had been brave. Ears! Don't talk to me about ears. I don't know which is worse, ear drops or the hair dryer at the dog groomer's. I had my fair share of gynae problems, too, until I was spayed and the mistress discovered evening primrose. That was a blow, knowing I would never have puppies of my own. I'd always attracted the attentions of the opposite sex, even Chablis, the haughty wine merchant's Labrador. I was the only bitch who could entice him off his front step. I don't know if dogs fancied my glossy white and chestnut coat, my smile or my wiggle but it's hard to stop a spaniel wiggling if she's pleased to see someone. Mind you, my mistress was very kind to me at that time and took me to the office whenever she could. I think she was having similar health problems of her own and the master was away a lot on business. I was able to develop my guarding skills, though I confess I did creep downstairs at my mistress's heels if she heard a noise at night.

Anyway, just as I hit middle age, bingo. They moved up to the moors! As soon as I put my nose out of the car window when we left Pickering I quivered with excitement. Rolling hills ablaze with heather, no fences, interesting patches of woodland, streams and those smells ... mmm. Damp earth, bracken, sheep, a hint of badger and rabbit and something new and tangy – grouse! It got better. We were to live near a river. In my youth I had jumped into an icy torrent in Devon and crossed the river to track a deer. The family were frantic but I've never forgotten it. It was even more exciting than following a herd in the snow, when I used to come home with ice balls in between my toes. Devon did have its downside, though, like the time the kids put me on a windsurfer and floated me out to sea, or when a gang of swans cornered me on the mud flats below the sea wall.

I was a fast learner where smells were concerned and the mistress helped, lobbing sticks and bones into thickets and hay meadows for me to find. She wasn't a bad trainer, not a patch on the gamekeeper at my field trials lessons but then he wouldn't have given me a cosy, warm bed next to the Aga, oh no, it would have been an outside kennel with no heating and all those yapping neighbours. I do like to be quiet sometimes.

Having a river a stone's throw away was a bonus. I could hear it burbling away at night, plus a few familiar squawks. When I got into the garden that first morning, I peered through the fence into the field and could scarcely believe my luck. It was crawling, simply crawling with pheasants. They were so tame they were almost too easy. My mistress took me on the lead over the stepping stones, which I quickly

learned to sprint across, where there were ducks bobbing about in the shallows, a heron and a couple of alarmed moorhens. I sniffed the breeze and detected a faint hint of otter and something rank, which turned out to be mink. Evil little devils but I did bring one home to show the family. They were not impressed as the body was a little high by that stage.

Yes, my prospects were transformed when we moved up here. Hunting and retrieving have been my life and it's given me a new sense of purpose. Now I sit by the fire and dream of those happy times on the moors. I'm told I twitch a little in my sleep. When I've got the old bones warmed up I climb upstairs to bed, which my mistress has thoughtfully placed on the landing directly over the hot pipes leading to the airing cupboard. So good for arthritic limbs – my joints aren't what they used to be after a lifetime of jumping. The family are still downstairs, watching TV but my hearing's on the wane and my eyes are dim. Bed's a good place for an old girl like me and I've got to get my beauty sleep. After all, they'll need me for picking up in the morning. I am proud to say there's nothing whatsoever wrong with my nose.

♦♦♦♦♦♦♦♦♦♦♦

The Last Jumble Sale.

Pat Almond

'Stuff' began arriving at the village school weeks before the event. It came in black bin bags, old suitcases, cardboard boxes and carrier bags. Gradually the heap spread through the building, invading classrooms, corridors, cloakrooms and the school office.

"What are we going to do with all this lot?" murmured Mrs Jackson the head teacher, "we shan't sell half of it!"

Every year in May the school held a jumble sale. Everyone in the locality knew the date and saved all their cast-offs as both a contribution and a way of getting rid of unwanted belongings. Work went on as usual, with the children becoming more and more excited as the piles grew. They became adept at peering into boxes and feeling the contours of bags as they squeezed past them on their way to lessons. One six year old boy was seen to rescue a green hippo sent to the sale by his mum without his knowledge. Mrs Jones turned a blind eye at the lump in his book bag as he scuttled from the building at hometime.

Two nights before the appointed day the big classroom was cleared of anything that could be sold by mistake, and the tables arranged down the centre of the room.

"Like locusts they are, buy anything," the caretaker grumbled as she interrupted her cleaning to peer into the depths of a pile of clothing.

Early on the day before the sale a group of Mums arrived to help set up the stalls. The children were confined to a stripped down infant room and given tables practice and colouring sheets to keep them occupied whilst the adults wrestled with their preparations. Two mums and one or two older children struggled up and down the stairs with all the jumble whilst the others sorted the contents; men's from women's, household from bric-a-brac, children's from grocery.

It had been decided at the Parents' Meeting that each helper could buy just one article before the beginning of the sale. It wasn't long before the first shriek of delight was heard, and one of the youngest mums nipped into the ladies to try on the dress she'd found.

"Get it Jill, it suits you," said one of the watching viewers as the outfit was paraded.

"Who sent that?" said another.

All eyes followed the school cook when she visited the sale room, in case she should escape with a treasure that was rightfully theirs. One bag of clothing was full of grubby underwear and dirty socks. It was hastily thrown out, the finder rushing to the cloakroom to wash away any taint with warm water and soap. Another bag yielded a red satin basque trimmed with lace, and a pair of large peach coloured bloomers.

"Who sent them?" asked one mum.

Catcalls and whistles greeted the comely lady who dared to try on both at the same time and mince down the corridor wearing them. Muffled laughter from the boys' toilets suggested that it made a welcome diversion for a couple of boys lurking there unseen.

Eventually everything was unpacked and the room transformed into a mountain range of old clothes. Children and parents wandered home chattering loudly and the secretary made tea for the teachers. On the office desk lay four lethal-looking carving knives, two videos of doubtful content and an illustrated copy of 'The Joy of Sex', rescued just in time from the hands of the seven year olds setting up the book-stall.

"Who sent that?" asked the secretary.

Come the morning of the sale the children assembled to spend their pocket money. Lots were drawn for who was to go first and spare cash rustled up for those who had nothing to spend. The six year old retrieved his hippo again for 50p, and one small girl headed for pink slippers with cats faces on the front. An eight year old dug out a pair of jeans she'd spied.

"Those were mine" said an older junior with a satisfied smile, only to see the younger child replace them quickly and buy a pair of high heeled shoes instead. Small teams of children, each allotted to a stall, counted out tubs of coins and practised giving change. Bulging bags of purchases were hung in the cloakroom for safe keeping.

After a hasty lunch all was ready. Adults were beginning to queue at the gate and the children had taken up their positions on the various stalls. Some were outside with books, shoes and the 'Take at your own risk' electrical goods. Some were on clothes, some selling cakes and old tins of chopped tomatoes on the grocery stall. A trusted few sold tickets for the raffle. Amongst the assembled grans and aunties was a well-known dealer from Pickering hoping to find a Fabergé among the frippery, and a farmer's wife with several shopping bags, respected as an excellent customer from previous sales.

When the bell rang at 2 o'clock they were off!. The buyers surged into the playground and up the stairs. Then it began to rain. The assistants in the yard rigged up a piece of plastic to keep themselves and their books dry. Potential buyers hurried inside and the rain ran unheeded into the shoes lined up for sale near the door.

The building was packed and hot, with the younger children soon becoming fractious. One buyer took her purchases home and then returned to ask for a refund on a 20p dress because 'it doesn't suit me'. The rest of the company dwindled into small groups of chattering families and then began to drift away. The piles of goods seemed undiminished by the buyers and the teachers retired for tea in the office and the counting of piles of small coins.

One eight year old returned later in tears having lost a jumper, presumably sold, and his friend accompanied him home wearing a two piece recognised as once belonging to his class teacher.

It was the last jumble sale. A tradition killed by the charity shops.

♦♦♦♦♦ ♦♦♦♦♦

Whitby Tales of Terror!

Jean Ramsdale

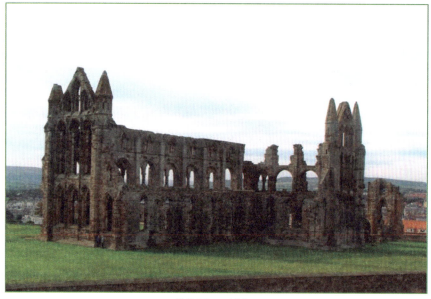

Whitby Abbey

*Ghosties, Ghoulies and bangs in the night
Don't venture out if you easily take fright
Tipping, Tapping, spine-chilling tales
Of Vikings. abbeys, sailors and whales!*

*See Cliff Street House where the Dutchman dangled
Whilst under the sea, St.Hilda's Bells jangled
And Headless Browne Bushell may make you take flight
If you dare to pass Bagdale Old Hall at night!*

*In St. Mary's graveyard lies the Hill of the Dead
Where the Black Bargeist coach by six horses led
Crashed into the grave, and ghouls three times passed round
The dead sailor's body, fresh in the ground!*

*Then off they drove wildly, down Henrietta Street
Their awful and gruesome destiny to keep*

So, on a haunting night that's no place to be
As you may be snatched as they crash into the sea!
If in Skinner Street you dare walk, late at night
You must watch out for a certain sight
Make haste and flee if you spy two black cats
Especially if they're wearing witches' hats!

In ancient Haggersgate, so it is said
The 'press-gangs' their grisly business led
And in certain dwellings, the spirits roam
Be careful and don't stay in Haggersgate alone!

High on West Pier a large Lighthouse stands proud
But only go in if you're part of a crowd
Beware on the stairs, as you may come to harm
As it's haunted by an old man with only one arm!

As my tales of the ghoulish make your soul shiver
Turn to the East, see the sun's rays quiver,
A sinister sight is seen in the sky
Beating its wings as it rises to fly
Back to the graveyard, its grisly work done
So, you'd better remember how to run!

We'll meet again, as I've more tales to tell
But I'm fleeing now, like a bat out of hell!

Ode to the River Esk
Judy Rawlinson

River of many moods, with grace
You slither down through gorge and field,
Unheeding, sliding, with quickening pace
    When to the sea your waters yield.

    You bubble through the peaty moor
    At birth, a spring alive and free.
    Slowly, streams gather, join and pour
        With greater force, rapidity.

Sheep sip from your clear pools, and birds
    Swoop low to drink, catch insects, fish
    Beneath the spreading skirts of trees
Which cloak your snaking, rippling swish.

    A salmon leaps to catch his prey,
    A silver crescent gleaming bright,
    Proud symbol of the fading day,
    While hooting owls salute the night.

    Your steady flow, so calm, so deep
    Is quickened by the storms that fall
On distant hills. The lightning's flash
    And thunder herald torrents, all
    Plunging in their murky dash.

The sun emerges, floods run dry.
Some ducks return to dabble anew.
You gently weave beneath clear sky,
Your surface sparkling, dappled, blue.

COLOURFUL CHARACTERS

In the Educational Psychologist's Chair
Jean Ramsdale

I dunno why you're bothering to talk to me, I'm a rebel and a problem teenager. It's all on me record, you've got it there and its too fat for the envelope now. All the teachers except Ms.Bond *hate* me, and I think that's great.

I'm the only girl in class who's dared to say 'F...you' to the teacher. I was suspended for five days - what a laugh, 'cos it's just what I wanted. Me friend Rosie got suspended at the R.C. School at the same time. We planned it brilliantly! Anyway, it was all worth it to see the English teacher's face. She lost her rag and the class cheered and went wild. I think it made the boy I'm after proud of me. I heard he's said I was cool - cool Kylie!

What yer asking me 'What did me and Rosie do for five days?'
E-a-s-y, we went to town shoplifting. We've done it before and never been caught yet! We know the game and act as look-outs for each other and then find a park or somewhere to share things. Naw, we don't pinch big things - where would we hide the stuff? We both made pouches in craft lessons 'specially to pin inside our skirts; the rest's easy - dodging the cameras is a scream, as long as there's two of us. The best marks I ever got was for making that pouch. Teacher said I was a *re-formed* character!

Why are you questioning me about me mam? Doesn't care about me. She's only thirty-three and has had *loads* of boyfriends. At least two are after her now. I haven't met them all, they change too quick for me to get home in time. She's always moaning that I hold her back but when she's had a good night out she comes into me room and says she loves me. Then the crying and stuff comes next. How would 'they' (dunno who she means) like to be a single mother. Anyway people say I look like her. I don't mind that 'cos she's got great legs and wears skirts up to her arse. She's 'with it' and sticks up for herself all the time - and I copy her.

What do yer mean 'Do I enjoy copying her?' Who else can I copy? The teachers are just a laugh, except for Ms. Bond. They're stupid and thick, expecting *me* to 'behave'. I'm a rebel and I look out for meself, no teacher or school is going to change *me*. I'm KYLIE and some of the kids look up to me - I like that.

What yer asking me about Ms. Bond for? Don't *you* know her? - you're the school shrink. You're supposed to know everything and make me into a good girl. No use asking me if *I* think I'm rude and cheeky, it only makes me worse. Haven't you got the message. *I - just - don't - care*! You can't put me away unless I'm violent and I'll watch that! Me mouth is what people are scared of.

Anyway, I thought you wanted to know about Ms. Bond. She likes me 'spirit' and when I feel 'disruptive' (her word, not sure exactly what it means) she lets me into her classroom at lunchtime. We practise 'meditation' (that's her word too) which does make me feel happier. It's simple - gets rid of me bad temper. Anyway, you're just like the rest of 'em. You aren't telling me the truth - why can't *you* make me feel good? Ms. Bond makes me feel okay again. She didn't like me at first 'cos I said 'Where's James?' (007, but I bet you haven't heard of him).

The trouble was I said it when one of those *Inspection* things was going on. She went bright red and ordered me outside the room. This Inspector man suddenly stopped looking bored and stared at me. If I hadn't felt sorry for Ms. Bond I would have said 'What yer staring at? I haven't got me nose ring in to-day!' But to me own surprise I muttered 'Sorry Miss,' and stamped outside, with just a medium banging of the door.

After that, Ms. Bond seemed to take notice of me. No-one knows that we sometimes talk - but if you sprag on me, I'll never come in this room again. You'd better not have a tape recorder either. If you try that one I'll make sure I get me worst swearwords in at the beginning. Anyway, I'm bored now and I've just seen you yawning and that's what's done it.

I expect you'll be back after I've been suspended again. It's up to me friend Rosie this time. I planned the last one! Have you met Rosie yet? She's got toe-rings and a belly button clip. She shows it to everyone she meets.

Just thought I'd warn you!!!

♦♦♦♦♦♦♦♦♦♦

Magic Kit

Pat Almond

Kit wasn't sure that he liked this new school. It was small and noisy with just two classes. He felt out of place here and longed for the high ceilings and corridors of the school he was used to in the town.

Mum said he would go back there once Gran was well but it was taking a long time. The cottage was cramped for the five of them. He liked the coal fire and the cat, though. The garden was good, too, with rows of cabbages and swedes and high trellises covered with beans.

He wasn't sure about Grandad. For a lot of the time the old man sat in a leather chair with worn patches on the arms, seeming to gaze into the fire for ages or just doze. When he wasn't in the chair he was out in the garden, weeding or hoeing or collecting vegetables for Mum to cook for them.

Kit was scared of Grandad's sadness. He didn't know what to do or what to say. The old man said very little but Kit could see it on his wrinkled face whenever he came down from Gran's room, where she lay propped on high pillows in the big bed beneath the window. Kit wasn't used to a man being there all the time. Dad was in the army and came home sometimes but usually it was just the three of them, Kit, Mum and baby Marie. Dad brought laughter with him but Grandad seemed to have lost his somehow.

When Gran was taken ill there was no-one else to help so the three of them had come to stay until Gran was better. Mum said he must go to school in the village but it didn't feel right. They were too close, too interested and he couldn't just slide away into a quiet corner when he didn't feel like talking. And now there was this special afternoon to deal with.

"We have a fun afternoon to celebrate Hallowe'en" said his teacher. "Everyone takes part, dresses up or something, it's great fun."

Kit wasn't so sure. Mum was busy all the time running up and down stairs and looking after the baby. He couldn't ask her to make a costume or find him something to take. He wished he was at home.

When he got back from school Mum was hanging out washing. Grandad was asleep in his chair so Kit lowered himself onto the rug and gently rubbed the ears of the tabby cat curled warmly on the hearth. He watched the leaping flames and was lost in his clouds of wishes.

"She's a good listener isn't she, Tabs I mean," said the old man quietly.

"But I haven't told her anything yet," Kit replied.

"Maybe not but she knows there's something on your mind…..I'm not a bad listener either….."

Kit felt the flickering warmth at his face and was aware of the darkening corners of the room as the daylight faded.

"Well it's Hallowe'en, Grandad. I don't know what to do, I can't ask Mum. I don't want to do anything here, I just want to go home." He felt Grandad's hand touch his hair, and it comforted him.

"Yes, lad, I expect you do, I expect you do at that," the old man said.

When Kit came home from school the next night Grandad beckoned him from the shed.

"Come over here lad, I've had an idea." They worked in the shed for the next few nights and by Wednesday even Mum had noticed.

"What are you two cooking up in that shed?" she asked. Kit smirked and Grandad chuckled,

"Nothing you'd want for tonight's tea that's for sure!" he said, winking at Kit.

Grandad was up early on Thursday and offered to walk Kit down to school. He waited at the gate until Kit was safely into the cloakroom clutching a big black shoebox under his arm. The Hallowe'en afternoon went well with children dressed as ghosts, skeletons, witches and other ghoulish things. One by one the children did their bits until it was almost hometime.

"Is it my turn?" Kit asked.

"Well yes Kit, I wasn't sure if you'd want to when you hadn't a costume."

"I have something else," he said, "something better." He crossed the room and brought his box in from the cloakroom.

"Is it a Hallowe'en Kit?" joked Richard Moor. "Get it - a Kit?"

When the older boys stopped laughing and all the faces were turned his way Kit drew a mat of grey cobwebs form the box. He and Grandad had collected it from the corners of the shed. He draped it all round his hands and with his strongest clearest voice began …

"Round about the cauldron go, in the poisoned entrails throw …" and as he listed all the ingredients for the witches spell he opened his cupped hands to reveal an amber-eyed toad crouched on his palm. Grandad had known just where to find it in the damp place under the water butt.

Nobody moved in the darkened classroom, and they listened wide eyed as Kit wove the spell with his words. When he had finished there was a moment of silence, then the teacher said she was 'stunned'.

There was new respect in the eyes of the children too.

"What better could we have than Shakespeare" said Mrs Jackson. "The best, the very best, well done Kit." Even Richard Moor said it was good.

Grandad met Kit at the gate.

"Well?" he asked.

"It was great, Grandad, great and they all listened. He didn't jump off my hand and the girl next to me went *ugh* when she saw the cobwebs and Mrs Jackson said Shakespeare was the best and I'd done well and ..." Kit talked and Grandad listened.

Mum watched them from the cottage, chattering away happily hand in hand, absorbed in what each other had to say.

"Magic" she said, "seeing them like that. Just magic." Then she went inside to put the kettle on.

Changing Times
Kate Trewren

Not far away you'll find a general store,
Once an oasis on this quiet moor.
But in recent years it's changed its tone,
Catering mainly for tourists; so locals moan.
The owner's tall and rather florid,
His hair is grizzled and his flesh is solid,
His wardrobe's dull, he wears mainly grey
And struggles through each weary day,
Lost in his thoughts and seeming unaware
Of the reasons that many go in there.
To the steady tick of a silent clock
He stares around and surveys his stock:
What sorrows, past or present, cloud his day?
What all-pervading dreams get in the way
Of greeting, talking, or meeting -
However short and fleeting -
His customers' requirements in a non commercial way?

Snowy

Kate Trewren

He should have been grey,
He should have been part of a community,
But he was destined to be a loner,
A focal point for birds of prey.

Tall trees, short trees, noble fir and pine,
Sycamore and lime trees etch the skyline.
These form the wood where Snowy built his drey,
A fluffy white squirrel who should have been grey.

Soft fur fluffed in the sunshine
Or white coat merging in snow,
A squirrel of unusual beauty
Watched the seasons go.

Feeding, feeding all the day,
Bark in January, buds and shoots in May,
Plus all year round the birdfood he'd raid
Surmounting all squirrel-proof strategies made!

Surveying his domain through pink, round eyes,
Perched atop the nut-globe, he'd soon devise
A way to get the nuts out with his sharp teeth,
To the chagrin of the pheasants, waiting nut-less beneath.

Or he'd hang from the feeder to spill out the seed,
(Which pheasants beneath gladly gobbled with greed.)
Then off at a scamper, away he'd dash,
Keen to establish a back-up cache.

Snowy graced the woodland for more than a year,
We were privileged to watch him, to get so near;
Yes, he was a rodent, a designated pest,
But of all our wild-life visitors, we loved him best.

Tall trees, short trees, noble fir and pine,
Sycamore and lime trees etch the skyline,
These form the woodland where Snowy built his drey,
A fluffy white squirrel who should've been grey.

No Job too Small

Judy Rawlinson

Me accountant says I'm not doing meself any favours if I don't put me rates up. Now, I know you're one of me oldest customers but I'm that busy, you wouldn't believe. I reckon I can fit you in, say, in a couple of month – how would that do, missus?

Aye, it's gone mad, as I say. Not like a few years back, when I started decorating. I'd lost me job at the mine when they cut the workforce by half. The pay was good but I never liked it there. Hot underground, with lots of dust and grease. Mucky work. The haulage ways used to creak and groan like a wild animal. That rock-breaking equipment and the noise, well, it took some getting used to. The shock wave just about blew you over when they blasted. What with wearing ear muffs, safety goggles, hard hat, boots, overalls and a lamp you felt like a spaceman. When I were on the back shift I never saw the light of day. Go down in the dark, come up in the dark, especially in winter. And I couldn't sleep during the day, oh no. The bairns saw to that, especially me youngest. After the colic it were teething, then when he started walking there were no peace. And we had four kids by then, to keep fed and watered, a mortgage to pay, instalments on the telly and the washer, a car to keep on the road. Have you ever tried using public transport up here? It's pathetic. I'd like to see Two Jags Prescott waiting for the bus on a freezing winter's morning, if it ever comes, that is.

Yes, I went down the mine because me dad wanted me to. He'd worked there for most of his life and I suppose he thought it was a good, steady job. Most of me classmates from school drifted in, sooner or later. So I served me apprenticeship and came out as a fitter, working on them machines. But I hated it. I never felt clean. And you were always with blokes, all the time, couldn't get away, not even at lunchtime. You sat down in a mucky corner with yer bait box and tucked in alongside yer mates. And it were like a madhouse when I came home, anyroad. No peace at all. It were doing my head in.

Then me wife got big ideas about wanting our house done up. I blame Changing Rooms and those other makeover shows on the telly. She had the plans but not the money. Anyway, when our youngest started school I fiddled about – never could sleep much in the day - and did out our kitchen and lounge while she was at work. It were great -

so peaceful, just the radio for company. I fitted the kitchen units – never thought of meself as a joiner but I couldn't afford to pay for one - did the tiling and the electrics but me favourite were the painting. Now, me wife fancied a few 'paint effects', she called 'em, so I did those and all – sponging, rag rolling, I had a go. She even wanted a lemon tree growing in the conservatory (I'd put one of those up for her, and all) so I said look, love, I'll do you one on the wall! And I did. It looked reet good, even though I says it what shouldn't.

Anyway, I lost me job and I had to earn summat, so I put an ad in the Gazette.

'Painting, decorating and general fixing. Clean, tidy worker. No job too small. Tel 01947 ……... any time.'

Well, sticking me home number down were a mistake, for a start. Our Kimberley would shout down the phone, things like "Yer what? Oo's this speaking, then?" then yell "Dad, it's for you!" or "He's down the pub." No I couldn't train me kids on customer relations. And 'any time' - I'll say, weekends, at bedtime, one o'clock in the flipping morning. I've learnt me lesson – I've got a mobile now and no one, but no one, gets me home number, present company excepted, of course.

When I started it were a struggle. Everyone was into DIY and that's it – they did it themselves. Besides, in this area folks didn't have the money. I'd paint a bedroom here, wallpaper the odd lounge, fix up some cupboards someone's husband had made a start on and botched up. Then I got me big breakthrough.

It were about five years ago, when people started coming up to the coast. Whitby was quaint, full of character, a timewarp – never mind that you couldn't find car parking - and the moors were on your doorstep. I got a call from a bloke who'd bought a farm up the valley and was doing up some barns for holiday cottages. He didn't live at the farm, like, he were a businessman and the place was his holiday pad. I think the holiday cottages were a little project for the missus, to keep her from being bored up here.

Anyhow, I pitch up with me tins, stepladder and brushes and get to work. At least they'd had a decent plasterer in so I got cracking. Mrs. Fanshawe were a right lady, always offering cups of tea and biscuits but she left me alone to get on. I were happy as a bee, slapping paint on – good stuff, too, Farrow and Ball colours she'd chosen, very tasteful – and listening to Classic FM on me radio.

Mrs. F came in, looking surprised.

"Sorry, missus, is this disturbing you?" I says. "I can put me headphones one, if yer like."

"No, Ken, it's just that I'm surprised. Decorators don't normally like classical music." I had to smile.

"Oh, aye, missus, I can't stand that modern stuff. What a racket. I have enough of that at home."

That job were a joy to do. Got on with it, just me radio for company and lovely views to look at out of the barn windows. When they put the ewes into the fields with the lambs, well, it would melt a heart of stone. When the weather got a bit warmer, I finished the woodwork outside, then. Mr. F came up from London one weekend and had a good look.

"You're doing a nice job there, Ken," he said.

When I took him into the pool area he was really taken aback. Oh aye, they'd put in an indoor pool and a jacuzzi for the punters, no messing. Mrs. F had wanted to put some big, jungly looking plants in there but I said they would take a lot of looking after. Why not, I says, have a picture on the end wall – of a jungle, if you like?

"What, you mean a *trompe l'oeil*?" she says.

"If you say so, love. I've done a lemon tree for the wife at home. Shall I give it a go? I can always paint over it if you don't like it."

So I goes ahead and there it is, a jungle, complete with tigers peeping out of the undergrowth, parrots and monkeys swinging from the trees.
Mr. F stands back and gets and eyeful of this wall. I could tell he was impressed.

"Well, Ken, that is amazing. A wonderful example of naïve art. I hope you don't charge extra for this," he joked.

"No, Mr. Fanshawe, same rate as usual."

After I'd finished in the barns Mrs. F asked me to do some work in the house. Victorian, it were, lovely moulded cornices on the ceilings, original chequerboard tiles in the hall. I got me ladders out and did some gilding and highlighting on those plaster mouldings. She got some wonderful wallpaper, too, Colefax and Fowler, reproduced from archive designs. So easy to hang, not like some modern stuff that falls apart in yer hands.

"You're an artist, Ken. I think you need to change your ad in the Gazette," says Mrs. F.

Since then I've never looked back. Everywhere you look now there's scaffolding, new building, extensions, conversions. There's hardly an old building left that hasn't been sorted out. There's so much work on that I've got five blokes working with me now, three I've trained up. Good lads, ones I can trust, though I does the fiddly bits meself still. Quality control, they call it. Mrs F even put together a

new ad for the paper, plus I do Country Living and Yorkshire Life now:
'Dales Design and Decoration'

We are specialist decorators who are experienced in the restoration and sympathetic decoration of period and traditional homes. All our work is done by highly skilled artisans. For a preliminary analysis of your requirements and a comprehensive estimate, please telephone 07773 …….. (mobile) from 6.30 pm to 8.30 pm, weekdays only.

Pheasants
Kate Trewren

His chestnut-brown plumage
Marked with cream and black,
The cock pheasant prances,
Almost dances – arrogance personified -
Whilst on her nest, his lady love
Undergoes enforced rest
Hatching her eggs.

The female pheasant made her nest
Beneath a leafless willow tree.
Shelter almost zero, privacy nil,
Just two yards from my washing line
She sat there, quite still,
Through wind and heavy rain.
Night, morning, noon and night again,
With falling pegs and marauding cat,
Through it all she sat and sat,
Neglecting her hunger, becoming bedraggled,
Her focus, her eggs, remaining unaddled.
I can't let her starve. Instead
Each day I feed her bread,
A token of female solidarity –
And she is not afraid of me.   *(over..*

Her quiet colours make her seem dull
In contrast to her mate,
Who struts pompously
Towards the bread, too late!
But still I fuss and remonstrate.

He's an iridescent sheen of purple and green
Below a red, featherless face.
Flapping scarlet wattles and erect ear tufts
Lend a hint of humour to his beauty.

I see vulnerability in his round, ginger eyes
As he hoots, like a train,
Charges along like a plane,
His runway, the lawn,
A noisy take-off.
Short flight – destination tree,
Silent landing.
He is afraid of me!

♦ ♦ ♦ ♦ ♦ ♦ ♦ ♦ ♦ ♦ ♦

The Fruit Baskets

Jean Ramsdale

The Fruit Farm proclaimed its existence with a giant eye-catching poster, FREE FRUIT AND GET PAID! Underneath the words, garishly painted, were huge sickly pink strawberries, elongated raspberries and artificially green gooseberries.

"It's slave labour down there," muttered one of the job centre customers.

"They'll wear you down. The only thing they don't have is a whip!" The short plump woman was turning red with indignation as she continued.

"If they try to send me there again I'll rebel. It put me off strawberries for life!" I couldn't help laughing to myself. It surely couldn't be that bad, and I did love fruit. I lost sight of the plump protestor in the general rush for jobs and found myself clutching a card with time and place in bold print. 'Temp summer job at Trenchers Fruit Farm'.

It was a cold, drizzling July day when the hired bus dropped us off at the fruit farm. During the ride a strident Scottish voice somewhere behind me was constantly raised above the general chatter. I guessed the voice belonged to a dark-haired, belligerent looking man. He seemed to have taken on the role of general protector of the ladies. The crowd of about fifty bodies seemed mostly to be women. A few men stood aloof and ignored the loud Scotsman.

Feeling lost, I followed the others towards the open door of the farmhouse. Standing by with a clip-board, was a big red-faced man. In an impressively resonant voice he yelled,

"Let's get you lot registered and picking! We want no hanky panky here. It'll be a fair day's pay for a fair day's work."

"It had better be!" Scotty's loud voice caught our ears and a thin-faced blonde nudged me.

"I think he's great - he'll see we get our rights," she whispered.

After a few days things settled down on the fruit farm. The thrill of freebie fruit soon grew stale and we needed the comradeship which the mix of personalities provided. The blonde had taken a shine to Scotty and to her he became our Labour Saviour. Scotty pursued his vendetta against the management and began to act uncannily like Peter Sellers in the film 'I'm All Right Jack'. Blondie admired and stuck by him, as daily he became more puffed up with self-importance. I sensed fireworks in the air and hoped the job would last as long as the fruit. As a struggling writer I needed the money and free fruit to survive.

Well, Scotty's importance continued to swell until the manager could no longer ignore him. There was a feeling of mutiny in the air when Scotty stood up and spouted, "We're being used as slave labour and made to look like fools." Blondie visibly flinched when a man's voice called out -

"Strawberry, Raspberry or Gooseberry Fools!"

Scotty went red-faced and grim-looking.

"We've got to negotiate our concessions. All we're getting is one midday break with some leftover squashed fruit. It's not good enough!"

The same man's voice called out,

"You've been eating too much fruit, Scotty - you're turning into a gooseberry!" Scotty didn't like being laughed at and turned to Blondie for support. To my astonishment she sidled away as the manager appeared.

"Right you lot, you're either here to work or you're out. The Job Centre has another list of fruit lovers queuing up to take your jobs. But you Scotty, we're letting you go – with a big raspberry!" With curses and threats of union sanctions, Scotty picked up his pay and stamped off.

"'Well Blondie, how are you going to manage without your soul-mate?" the manager leered. Blondie ignored him, turned away and walked with me to the picking field.

"You know, I thought Scotty and me were an item, but I found out two days ago that he's also been taking out that po-faced brunette from the Job Centre. No-one does that to me and gets away with it!" With a spiteful look on her face she spat out, "I spragged on him and told the Farm Owner his secret plan." Blondie had now made me curious.

"What was his secret plan?" I asked.

"Well, he was going to persuade us to sit down on the fruit for as long as we could last whilst singing 'Keep the red flag flying'. "Anyhow," she continued, "I've found out he's off to Cuba soon, someone told him that Fidel Castro is recruiting grape-pickers with a 'special bonus' at the end!"

I decided my fruit-picking days were over. Starve or not, I was not intending to turn into a fruit basket.

THOUGHTS FROM ABROAD

Where the Water Meets the Sky
Judy Rawlinson

It was almost two months since we had arrived at our new home in the African bush. The strangeness of my surroundings was beginning to fade but not my longing for the animals we had left behind in England.

Mum realised I was missing our pets. My longing intensified when we were invited out of town to a *braaivleis* (barbecue) evening at Bahati, a manganese mine in the forest. The Australian manager and his wife lived in a large house with a brood of six children and a menagerie of animals. They occasionally came to the Club for a film or tennis tournament in their sturdy American station wagon, lying the kids down to sleep like sardines in the back. They were a jolly lot, always bursting into song. "Come on, kids, join in!" the father cried as he pulled out of the car park.

> "Roll along, Land Rover, roll along,
> For it's time we were singing you a song.
> Mufulira may be fine
> But give me Bahati Mine,
> Roll along, Land Rover, roll along!"

There was a lot of singing – and drinking – at the party. Besides the Land Rover song we had The Wild Colonial Boy, The Foggy, Foggy Dew and Waltzing Matilda. The grownups drank and drank and grew maudlin. Mum shot Dad a look which said 'Time we were going, Jack' but, as usual, he took no notice. Oh, no! They were singing 'I'll Take You Home Again, Kathleen'; always a bad sign.

I wandered into the garden to take a closer look at the animals. There were dogs, cats, monkeys, birds, two bushbuck who picked their way through the house on dainty hooves and two tame warthogs, Mildred and Stewart, who drank from the waterhole on their knees. One of the cats had produced a litter of kittens. I was asked, would I like one? She was a pretty little thing, tortoiseshell and affectionate.

We took her home that night. As I cuddled and soothed her on my lap, stroking the soft fur, I decided to call her Mimi. Only a week or so later Jean asked, "Would you like to go to Samfya?" We were walking down to the grocery store in town. Jean, barefoot, scuffed the dust with her toes.

"Where's that?"

"It's on the big lake. It's like the seaside. There's white sand, you can swim. Dad fishes there sometimes. Maybe he could take us one Sunday." Guy, however, was not to be persuaded. He only got one day a week off – Sunday – and he wasn't going to sacrifice it to spend a few hours driving up and down a bumpy bush road so that his daughter could have a swim. His buddy who owned the boat wouldn't be there, anyway. What did he want to sit on a beach for? He would rather continue his romance with the gin bottle at home.

"Ask your dad," Jean wheedled, "Maybe he could take us?"

"It's no good, Jean, he doesn't have a car. He doesn't even have a government Land Rover."

Samfya was a government station of nine houses and offices on the shore of Lake Bangweulu. It was popular with families for a day out or a weekend's camping and, over long holidays like Rhodes' and Founders' (Rogues and Scroungers) weekend, townies would come up from the Copperbelt, 150 miles away.

Dad knew I was longing to go. One morning I opened the door to one of his African clerks, bearing a chit saying 'Jude, Get your swimsuit and towel out - Mr. Ogden has to deliver some stores to Samfya. He'll be collecting you and Jean at 9.30! Love, Dad.' I rushed off to the bedroom and grabbed my things, plus a gin bottle of squash from the fridge and two bananas. I was ready.

Mr. Ogden, one of the PWD foremen, pulled up in his Bedford vanette, with Dad and Jean on the bench seat alongside him. Oh no, he'd brought his wretched dog along, a bull mastiff cross. Mr. Ogden looked like his dog: he was brisk, burly, with a moustache and red face. The Africans called him Bwana Shout. As I stood on the front steps the dog leapt out of the back of the vanette and shot across the drive where my young cat recoiled, ears back, frantically looking for a tree to climb. She never made it. The dog pounced and seized the terrified creature by the scruff of her neck, shaking her like a rat. We ran towards the dog and Mr. Ogden grabbed his collar. Mimi, dripping with blood, crawled into the undergrowth.

"Don't worry, Jude," said Dad. "She'll be fine. You go. You must go. Jean will be so disappointed if you don't." I knew my cat would not be fine but I got into the vanette. Mr. Ogden, the pig, was now in the passenger seat and made us two girls sit in the back. He wanted his African driver at the wheel for the Samfya road was treacherous, narrow and sandy, with patches of black cotton soil where it crossed the *dambos,* swampy areas. Mr. Ogden wanted to be chauffeured in style. He had a load of bricks, oxygen cylinders and sacks in the back but we would add extra weight, to make the vehicle more stable. Chivalry was a word alien to Mr. Ogden's vocabulary. Perhaps he felt ashamed about his dog and couldn't face us. I didn't know and I didn't care.

That journey and my first view of the lake passed in a mist of tears. We slithered along the road and were soon choking on fine, white dust. We sat on sacks and put scarves over our noses and mouths, like bandits. Naked children gazed open-mouthed as we drove past villages, the older ones waving, as their mothers pounded millet. Long-legged chickens ran in front of the vanette and escaped with their lives. Women were hoeing small plots of land dotted with tree stumps, straight-backed, digging the blade backwards between their toes and others walked gracefully along the road, carrying huge bundles of wood on their heads. We passed the Samfya airstrip, climbed a long hill and there it was, Bangweulu, 'where the water meets the sky'. The turquoise waters close to the shore deepened into cobalt as they merged with a clear blue sky on the horizon. The lake was dazzling.

Mr. Ogden dropped us off at the small, deserted beach, below the clutch of bungalows on the hill, while he went off to the local PWD stores. We changed into our swimsuits behind some trees, inhaling the musky smells of wild jasmine and the herbs that dotted the sand dunes. A gentle breeze rustled the papyrus reeds fringing the beach. Apart from the slap, slap of wavelets on the clean, white sand, there was silence. We looked as white as a pair of ghosts after the dusty journey but we ran into the lake, our feet squeaking on the dry sand. We gasped as it burned the soles of our feet and plunged into the delicious, cool water, washing the dirt from our bodies and some of the sadness from our souls. The water was clear and little minnows nibbled our toes but I felt too miserable to appreciate this new experience.

We only had an hour or two before the journey back. We were sleepy and hardly noticed the bouncing of the truck as we bucketed homeward in the lengthening shadows of the brief, African dusk. The dambo reeds glowed red in the twilight as we passed and we spotted two buck hesitantly pick their way to the stream to drink. They lifted their heads on slender necks and regarded us with their soft eyes, petal ears flickering. Egrets stalked around like large, white moths on legs as the sun sank before us, a burnt orange ball in the dusty haze.

It was dark when we turned into our drive. I didn't need to ask what had happened to my kitten. I looked at Dad and he shook his head silently. It had been a sudden, violent death, the first of many I would see in Africa.

Venice - La Serenissima

Pat Almond

"Overcrowded, overrated, overpriced – and it smells."

A verdict on Venice, yet still I wanted to go! Managing to find a flight and a small central hotel in the Airtours brochure, for just over £300 each, we left Manchester for La Serenissima on May 23$^{rd.}$.

To chug gently into the waterways of this beautiful place for the first time is an unforgettable experience. As we travelled by boat from Marco Polo airport to our hotel we were struck by the soft, mellow ochres and corals of the buildings lining the canals, the bridges and the many marble churches on either side of us. Once settled into our hotel we set out wanting only to drink our fill of Venice's beauty and absorb its unique atmosphere. The barman in a small café next to the hotel obligingly removed the top from a bottle of white wine and provided us with three plastic cups. We toasted our holiday watching a deep blue dusk fall over the lagoon from the steps outside the Doge's Palace.

Our beds were comfortable, the shower worked and the coffee was hot so after breakfast we began our exploration of the city. Venice is a feast for the senses. The absence of cars removes the grey backdrop of noise, despite traffic on the canals, and everyday sounds take on a new clearer quality. Elaborately decorated palaces fringe the water, but it is the quality of light and the peach and gold tones of the walls, that give the buildings their distinctive flavour. The whole city feels like a huge film set.

We bought a three day pass for the *vaporetto*, which gave us unlimited access to all areas of the city, and heard three versions of a Pavarotti favourite from passing gondoliers before even leaving the jetty! We cruised up the Grand Canal, seeing the Accademia, Rialto and all the other places we had read about. The waterway was thronged with barges carrying all the everyday goods necessary to sustain life in a city with no vehicle access and busy with water taxis and other small boats. Leaving the canal we wandered back to the hotel through sunlit alleyways and across quiet squares, meeting very few other visitors.

We were surprised by the number of people in the Piazza and round the central area when we returned in the late afternoon, as it had been quiet in the morning. This, then, was an area to avoid during the day as many visitors come on daily excursions and gather there. We found a small *trattoria* away from the Piazza, where we enjoyed a meal that cost much the same as its equivalent in Scarborough. During the day we found *una ombra*, literally a glass in the shade, a perfect lunch, comprising a soft sandwich and a glass of local wine at the counter of a bar. Cappuccinos at regular intervals provided sustenance and entertainment as we watched the passing show.

The advantage of staying in the city was clear by mid-evening. In St Mark's Square we joined a small crowd of onlookers to watch two violinists in one of the café orchestras shake off their sedate image and loosen into jazz, swing and fast folk music, to the delight of everyone there. Standing in the warm evening, against the backdrop of the domes and mosaics of St Mark's, enjoying the musicians' high spirits was a magical experience

We 'did' the Campanile on the following day, climbing high above the city and looking over on the domes that create the cross on which St Mark's is fashioned. The view was spectacular, and we could see out over towards the Adriatic, past the church of San Giorgio Maggiore and right along the Grand and Giudecca canals. Strangely these are the only canals visible from the rooftops, all the others being concealed between the buildings by their narrowness.

Later we crossed the lagoon to visit the Venice Lido and were startled by the reappearance of traffic. A smallish holiday town, with wired beaches reminiscent of the Normandy Landings, it nevertheless had a relaxed air to it and we ambled happily up the sunlit avenues that dominate the centre and enjoyed another spot of people watching. The journey back to St Mark's with its skyline lit from the sea, make this journey a must. The cathedral mosaics are lit each day for a brief period and at this time the crowds become impenetrable. By visiting late in the afternoon we missed some of the congestion and were able to savour the musty eastern flavour of the basilica and enjoy gazing up into '..the heaven contained inside a dome…'

On our final day we took the *vaporetto* out to the now defunct naval dockyard at Arsenale. The boat had to scrape with grinding jolts through the shallow approach way, and we were able to look through the elaborate gate to the little seaward entrance where the boats built there were released into the ocean. The skill of the Venetian boat builders provided the means by which the city's adventurers and explorers became successful. It also provided the ability to fashion the intricate lead domes of St Mark's, which were made here. Rounding the 'back' of the city en route to the glass makers' island of Murano we chanced upon a tableau of life in modern Venice. In the space of a few hundred yards, we saw a coffin being unloaded down the hospital ramp; a 'new' father going up the stairs above with an armful of flowers in the shape of a crib, a gondola decorated with gladioli complete with bride and groom, and a funeral barge making slow graceful progress on its way to the cemetery on the island of San Michele! It served as a reminder that Venice is a thriving real community, not just a tourist curiosity.

On our return we visited the Doge's Palace, mounting the Scala d'Oro to the map room. On the rough outline of North America drawn on the ceiling, the eastern seaboard and Florida were joined by a section marked 'Unknown'. This really brought home to us the courage of Venice's explorers, and reminded us that many of the city's treasures were plundered items brought home by its most famous sons. We visited the cells adjoining the Palace, crossing the infamous Bridge of Sighs, and were chilled to contemplate the arm rings in the wall that held prisoners secure even at high tide when water from the lagoon flooded the prison. Many prisoners survived only to be executed. All written information boards in the Palace feature a number of languages. We felt the English had probably been done by a professor of linguistics who enjoyed big words without necessarily understanding them, and it afforded us great amusement and helped temper the chill of the prison.

We left the city reluctantly. Venice is overcrowded, especially in the centre at peak times. The shopping was wonderful and whilst some things could be very expensive generally it was less so than London. In May rank smells from the canals were not a problem. Is Venice overrated? Not for me, I can't wait to go back.

To Rome and Back

Ann Bowes

There were times, especially as I packed my suitcase, when I thought it was all a dream. After all, I could count on one hand the times that I'd been out of Yorkshire. Abroad, never! For a while, as we waited anxiously for the coach in Whitby, I thought I wasn't going to Rome. No one informed us there'd been a change of plan and that we should have been at a different venue. Thanks to the mobile phone, we made it with minutes to spare and after a long trip to Heathrow and two hours of endless queues, security checks and officialdom, were summoned to board. I experienced my first flight with a mixture of apprehension, wonder and excitement. It was midnight when we touched down and walked out into the balmy Italian air. A coach was waiting to transport us to the Ergife Palace Hotel on the Via Aurelia, on the outskirts of Rome. Inside the huge ground floor reception area I was greeted by my niece, Sue, who had promised to look after me. We had been allocated different flights according to postal codes so I was very relieved to see her.

So this was Rome, the Eternal City. I gazed out from my balcony the next morning to see blue skies and a sun already well up. Yes, I was really here. Sue and I were part of a diocesan pilgrimage and knew our days would be packed with a busy schedule. We had all been allocated to one of four coaches and ours was the blue one. By 8.30am we had breakfasted and were on the coach to go to St. Peter's Square for the papal audience. We walked the short distance from the coach park, mingling with people from all nationalities and took our allocated seats. Although I had seen the pope give his Easter Blessing on T.V., I was not prepared for the vastness of the place. There are huge pillars in the semi-circular high stone walls on either side of the square, which connect to the massive façade of the Basilica with its enormous bronzed door in the centre. One hundred and forty stone statues of the martyrs and saints look down on the square from their lofty positions high on the walls and in the centre of the square stands the huge Vatican obelisk. Gazing up, I saw the majestic dome, one of eleven, forming part of the roof of this, the largest church in the world. After waiting two hours, we witnessed the frail figure of the pontiff in his pope-mobile, waving to all, as he was driven round the roped gangways between the hundreds of people who had amassed there to see him.

After the audience, we spent our free time soaking up the atmosphere of that great metropolitan city. We explored the narrow streets, the broad, bustling thoroughfares and saw endless pizza bars, street cafés, ice cream parlours and restaurants. Balconies and window boxes were ablaze with colourful flowers and exotic plants. All the while there was the noise of the traffic, horns continually hooting and scooters whizzing in and out between the cars like maniacs. We quickly learned to step out on to the road at crossings, as the vehicles only stop if there is someone actually on the road, which, at first, was a bit scary. Time flew and we hurried back to the coach depot where, in the mêlée, Sue and I became separated. I panicked momentarily but had to continue and hoped that she hadn't been left behind. Fortunately, we were reunited when we all disembarked at the Church of Perpetual Succour for our daily mass. After the service it was back to the hotel in time to wash and dress for dinner.

Each day we attended mass in a different church and visited many places. Our guided tour to the outside of the Colosseum (which is only open to the public on certain days) so impressed me that I was determined to return. A group of us walked back another day and entered that amazing stadium. I was transported back in time as I explored that huge arena. Looking below walkways I could see the iron bars across the entrance to the underground passageways and sensed the fear of death, the smell of caged animals and almost hear the roar of the frenzied crowds, baying for blood. On that hot sunny day I shivered inwardly. Although the completion of this amazing structure took seven years, it was still an achievement of great magnitude. Some of the stones were at least eight foot long and in its heyday there was even a movable ceiling to pull over. Without the availability of modern day machinery, what was accomplished was truly astounding. No wonder it became the symbol of the city and its life.

Our visit to The Catacombs left a lasting impression on me. Although never one to explore underground, I was totally relaxed and unafraid as I ventured down with our guide into that fourteen-mile maze of burial chambers, two and three storeys below the ground. Dimly lit and strangely quiet, the passageways are still as they were nearly 2,000 years ago. Painted stones and plaques depicting people and events from the bible are set in the walls. The long corridors contain dug-out tombs where the bodies would be laid and sealed with tiles or marble slabs. Leading off the galleries are small chambers, which are loftier tombs where whole families of note are interred. Many popes and martyrs are buried in these ancient cemeteries and became places of worship for the early Christians. There are larger rooms or chambers known as crypts, a notable one being where all the popes from the third century are buried. It wasn't eerie or chilling and a feeling of reverence and dignity pervaded the whole place. I felt a bond with those early Christians and felt a link with the faith that has been handed down through the generations. Our very simple but intimate mass in one of those burial chambers was perhaps the most inspirational moment of my visit to Rome.

In sharp contrast to our visit to the catacombs was our tour of the Vatican museum. After standing in the long queue in the street, we were eventually led into the huge reception area where we followed our guide through a series of rooms and hallways, each one more resplendent than the previous. There were sculptures, busts and statues of every shape and size, murals and paintings as well as large frescoes and tapestries. There were ancient maps, coins and medals. We viewed an endless display of art and history as we trod the marble floors beneath those ornate and decorated ceilings. Our tour ended in the Sistine Chapel, a place of wonderment, where silence is supposed to reign but despite the efforts of the guards, voices of every tongue could be heard in appreciation of the marvellous works of Michelangelo. I found it all a little overwhelming and was glad to be back outside in the open air.

Our pilgrimage embraced visits to sites of ancient Rome, which included the Forum, the Baths of Caracalla, the enormous Arch of Constantine and the House of the Vestal Virgins. We explored the Temples of Saturn and Vespasian and the enormous Circus Maximus below the Palatine Hill where the famous chariot races were held, also the well-preserved majestic Pantheon.

We visited many churches and basilicas, including St. John's, the first one to be built in Rome, that houses five altars. Another, which includes the Twenty Holy Steps reputedly shipped over from Jerusalem, also others containing the tombs of different popes and saints. We explored the many Piazzas with their fountains, climbed up to the roof of the Castel Sant' Angelo with its amazing views of Rome. We strolled by the Tiber, dark and brooding, flowing continually by, witness to events that made this city the capitol of a famous empire. I saw but a glimpse of Rome's history but a sense of the power and glory of its past will stay with me forever. I only have to look at my photos to know it wasn't a dream, but back in rural Yorkshire those days in the Eternal City now seem like a time in another life.

♦♦♦♦♦♦♦♦♦♦

The State of Florida

Pat Henderson

The State of Florida - is it in a state? Could this state of sunshine and pleasure be slowly killing the goose that laid the golden egg? A few people seem concerned but why spoil these halcyon days? We'll worry about it tomorrow!

As a frequent visitor over the past ten years, with family in an area called Riverview, I have watched an ever-increasing concrete jungle emerge. Just how many more conurbations can be squeezed on to swathes of green land? The obvious allure of warm days bathed in sunshine tempts many to leave the chill of northern winters but surely soon there will be nothing to enjoy but urban sprawl.

Fly to Florida for the vacation of your dreams! Enjoy its beaches of silky silver sand. Pick up exotic, pretty shells. Bathe in the warm seas but take care - at certain times of the year pollution can be dangerous. It's hard to believe the aquamarine waters harbour algae that can cause problems to health. As other idyllic tropical resorts become available worldwide, together with cheap flights, will tourists still come to Florida or be tempted by paradise elsewhere? Ah, but Florida has Disney World - everyone comes to enjoy Disney, don't they? The Fun Park, Universal Studios, Animal Kingdom, it's all there but new exciting theme parks (Disneyland included) are opening in other parts of the world. Could it be that Disney Florida will eventually lose its glamour and glitter? Of course not, it couldn't ...could it?

Visitors always enjoy seeking out creatures in their natural environment. Those that live in the Everglades thrill and excite - an alligator snoozing by a swamp or gliding with barely a ripple through the still murky water, turtles dipping and diving, a snake curling round a mangrove tree. However, already half the original Everglades has been eliminated and the food chain shrinks daily. When there is no longer a natural ecosystem due to the phenomenal rate of building, what will become of the flora and fauna? Guess it will never get as bad as that? Think again! Drainage, continual development and pesticides take their toll every day.

Have you ever watched raccoons, opossums and foxes in the twilight? They come into the yard to play and seek food which is often put out for them.* This actually helps to stop them raiding the trash-cans and disposes of polluting garbage. Raccoons are fascinating, their antics delightful, and they produce a litter of one to six babies a year. Although they will raid nests and steal eggs their main diet is of insects, small mammals, snakes, fruit and grubs - a natural balance of nature. However, with the ever-encroaching building programme their land is diminishing and they become urban pests who raid anything and everything just to get food.

Is it not time the people of Florida said enough is enough? Perhaps, for some, life is purely motivated by the seeking of pleasure and over-indulgence. We all have dreams of a beautiful home, a lifestyle in which the piggy-bank never empties and happiness prevails in the Sunshine State forever. Still, dreams can turn to nightmares and, though it may take generations, the outcome could be just that... a nightmare. A concrete jungle with small pockets of swampland drained of life-giving water and the indigenous wildlife gone forever from this unique part of America.

Think hard, think long, but not for too long, please!

(* The writer believes it has now become illegal to feed indigenous animals in suburban areas.)

♦ ♦ ♦ ♦ ♦ ♦ ♦ ♦ ♦ ♦ ♦

FANCIES, FRIENDS AND FEELINGS

Little Blue Book of Faded Autographs
Jean Ramsdale

You lay there, underneath papers long ago discarded as useful. Nestling amongst the packets of yellowing duplicating paper and blue carbon, fading away into antiquity. I never realised I still had you - so many life-changing events since you were part of my life. Before looking into your forgotten mysteries I have to make a cup of strong tea. Dare I hope that you may have something to offer me?

Inside front cover:
Well, why did I stick a good-luck stamp at the beginning and when I was only thirteen years old? Perhaps a premonition for the future....
Written underneath:

Jean Chapman - don't recognise my thirteen years old handwriting. However, the years passing since my divorce are starting to make my maiden name look familiar again. Hey! This shouldn't be about me, it should be about you, too.

You
Your blue cover edged with blurred gold looks so innocent. It's hurting me to look down on you. Your era was simple, uncomplicated and these names prove it.

May, Lily, Thelma.
I don't know you all since we left school. Have you all paid the price for your mistakes. Or are your faces unlined and serene, from an uneventful lifestyle?

Jacqueline
I know you've had troubles. Like black snowballs, hitting hard straight on target. You recognised me after all these years, and your

eyes are still a gorgeous luminous blue. Jacqueline, I wasn't looking out for a middle-aged woman pushing a wheelchair. Your son is a big man and only your amazing mother love gives you so much strength. You say he gives you 'unqualified' love and then, sighing, add your daughter is 'difficult' and has gone out of your life.

Roberta

Don't know how you've matured. When you married the local 'heart-throb' he whisked you off to South Africa. Heard you were proud of your large house, servants and swimming pool. Did you get the best treatment in South Africa for your breast cancer? I hope you got a good surgeon and that all went well. I would have loved to have seen you on one of your visits home. Why did you meet Sheila and not me, we were a trio?

Shirley

My prayers will have thoughts of you in them tonight. Forty is too young to die. I'm glad your husband was so loving and supportive. Your children's verses in the local paper were a tribute to your mother love.

Now Me! (unsigned)

He who fights and runs away, lives to fight another day.

Why did I choose these words for my own contribution? Did I have a premonition about the many times I would have to bounce back?

Little Blue Book, I'm glad I found you!

Singing.

Pat Almond

Singing nearly drives me mad,
Turns my eardrums red,
Leaving little snips of melody
Dancing through my head.

I go about my daily chores
Bright splinters in my mind,
Waves and waves of lovely sounds
Blue chords of ev'ry kind.

Bits I can't get rid of
Monopolise my thinking -
They fill my mouth at mealtimes,
It's quavers that I'm drinking.

Sometimes it's the main line,
Sometimes the refrain,
Little tuneful sunbursts
Exploding in my brain.

I hum the whole songs over
To make them go away.
Perhaps if they are once complete
Then that's the way they'll stay.

But still the phrases stick with me,
The sound swells through my heart,
It fills my ears, sticks in my teeth
And rips my skull apart.

I've tried and tried to wipe it out
But erasure's not the thing,
I'll have to find a quiet spot
And sing and sing and sing!

Games we Played

Jean Ramsdale

Games we played when we were six
Were sometimes done with *Tins and Sticks*
The ones before, I can't recall
Except I seemed to always fall
Perhaps the *Leapfrog* proved too wide
And in mid-air, I missed the ride.

      When *Statues* on the menu came
      I felt the need to claim some fame.
      Lone Ranger's horse I chose to be
      Neighing, prancing, wild and free.
      Sad, no one guessed my alibi
      As I galloped onto mountains high –
      To win you had to 'freeze' when told,
      Difficult with a horse so bold.

The *Tigger* game had lots of go
As frantically we'd to and fro,
Madly dashing here and there,
Avoiding 'tigs' as a mad March hare,
Too many tigs and you were out,
Slinking off, to your rivals' shout.

      The *Whips and Tops* came round once more
      And over chalk box we would pore,
      The reds, blues, greens and purples
      Flashed on tops which madly hurtled,
      Bashing next door neighbour's nose
      When slicing through some clean-washed clothes.

Sedately then we changed our tack,
Decided *Skipping Ropes* were back,
But not to skip, I must explain……
It's to the lamp posts we next laid claim,
The dads 'roped-in' to fix on high
A splendid rope with 'sailor's tie',
The thrilling feel of a flying ride

Was damped, to quickly run and hide
From a bobby clumping down the street
To catch the *'Lamp posters'* on his beat,
Forbidden was the rope on post
'Catch us if you can' we'd boast!

> When childhood times we left behind
> The grown-up games were brought to mind
> The first of these was *Dance Shotese*
> The fun in this were the boys we'd 'squeeze'

With childhood gone, things weren't the same
We were too cool to play the game.

♦ ♦ ♦ ♦ ♦ ♦ ♦ ♦ ♦ ♦

Tomorrow Will You Remember?
Jean Ramsdale

You once sported flares and I donned minis,
Just look at us now in overalls and pinnies.
Gazooks, what happened to our youthful style?
Now, we only dress-up once in a while!

Your hair has gone grey and mine is dyed fawn,
We stay in most nights, watch TV and yawn.
Should we try to recapture whatever we lost
Or will it all come at too much of a cost?

Do you think my pins still stand up in a mini?
Will Oxfam flares make you look a ninny?
Your grey thatch we'll cover with Nice 'n' Easy,
Though the resultant colour may look quite queasy.

No! It's all a dream, it cannot be -
We've over-indulged on reality T.V.

♦ ♦ ♦ ♦ ♦ ♦ ♦ ♦ ♦ ♦

Words of Consolation
Ann Bowes

On Reaching Forty

They say that life begins at forty
No matter what you've done,
So was the past a waste of time
Or just a practice run?
If so, don't be disheartened
And feel all sad and glum!
For practice makes for perfect
So the best is still to come!

For our Friend

They say that time's a healer
And that pain will fade away
But the memories we hold so dear
Are with us every day.
Think only then of good times,
Let sad thoughts disappear.
For although we cannot see him
We know he's always near,
The memory of his laughter
And times we all have shared
Will always be remembered
By the ones who truly cared.

Loss of a Son

No words of comfort can I find
That will help to ease your pain,
To lose a child is living hell and only
Heaven's gain,
So think of him in a better place
And the glory he has won
And console yourselves that you were blessed
To be given such a son

On Listening to Wagner (played too loudly)
Kate Trewren

It's all too dark;
All too dreary;
Hopeless hope is all around.
We strive to live,
But cannot give,
Inside such all-pervasive gloom.
There is no room
For spiritual fulfilment:
Shadows shade every glimmer,
Every bubble in the simmer
Of the turmoil of emotions
Boiling up to state our cause –
Liberation and such notions
Ground to nothing, nothing.
Life's a pause,
A hiatus of waiting
For the rule of others.

♦♦♦♦♦♦♦♦♦♦

How Do I?
Jean Ramsdale

How do I rest easy
When my mind is awash
With words?

How do I banish
Illuminating images?
It's hard.

How do I walk with friends
And keep my notebook
Out of sight?

How do I say
I haven't become a writer
Overnight?

How do I forget
The months and years
Of graft?

How do I explain?
I'll just say it's called
My craft.

BILBERRY PIE

Bilberries are damson blue, the size of redcurrants, with a misty, peachlike bloom. You are lucky to find these small fruits on the North Yorkshire Moors: they grow on low, ground-hugging bushes, surviving on poor soils and in harsh weather.

Pigeons like them as much as we do. Picking bilberries is time-consuming but if you can tolerate the flies and don't mind purple hands the effort is well worthwhile. The best bilberry pies have a juicy, tangy filling and are covered with a crisp but succulent pastry crust. We hope you enjoyed ours.

Our generous sponsors

The Scarman Trust

A great place to live, work & play

Scarborough Borough Council

Moors and Coast Committee of North Yorkshire County Council

Awards for All